My teacher's my friend, and I guess you could say
I've got all kinds of reasons for feeling this way.

She greets us each morning
on the playing field grass.

She helps us line up
and march into class.

The next thing we know,
we're singing a song
while our teacher chimes in
and sings right along.

We pledge our allegiance
with our hands on our hearts.

We dance all around
just to loosen our parts.

Once she's called roll
    to find out just who's there,
our teacher pulls up
    her storybook chair.

And nobody tells
    a story so well.

But then it's our "busy bee"
    time of the day
when everyone goes
    their own separate way.

And each of us has
    a job we must do,
like "lights-and-door helper"

and "paper helper" too.

So we march all around
in an organized spin
till everyone's ready
for the work to begin.

We paint pictures with sponges
of all different shapes.

We make clever posters
with scissors and tape.

We even dress up
        in the funniest ways
    to discuss big events
        and observe special days.

Then all of us honor
    the "star of the week"
as one of us gets up
    to share and to speak.

And one thing we've learned
    is we all get a turn.

Teacher shows us a movie
every once in a while.

She brings in guest speakers
to share things worthwhile.

She even takes care,
   when somebody cries,
to smooth out their problems
   and help dry their eyes.

My teacher's amazing,
I have to admit.
She helps us to spell.

She helps us stay fit.

And when the day's done,
without any fuss,
she guides us outside
to find the right bus.

Yes, she's there when we need her,
from beginning to end.

My teacher's my leader . . .

My teacher's my friend.